UP
JUMP
THE
BOOGIE

UP JUMP THE BOOGIE

POEMS BY JOHN MURILLO

CYPHER BOOKS

NEW YORK, NEW YORK

CYPHER BOOKS

310 Bowery
New York, NY 10012
info@cypherbooks.org / www.cypherbooks.org

Grateful acknowledgment is made to the editors of the following publications
in which these poems appear, sometimes in different versions:

> *Amistad:* "Up Jump the Boogie"
> *Beltway Quarterly:* "Dream Fragment With a Shot Clock and Whistles In It" (as "Point"),
>   and "Soon I'll Be Loving You Again" (as "Invoking Marvin at Midnight")
> *Callaloo:* "Variation on a Theme by Eazy E"
> *Cave Canem VIII:* "Dream Fragment With a Shot Clock and Whistles In It" (as "Point")
> *Cave Canem IX:* "Stolen Starlight Lounge Sutra"
> *Columbia Poetry Review:* "Enter the Dragon"
> *Court Green:* "Monster Boy" and "1989"
> *Florida Review:* "Renegades of Funk"
> *Lumina:* "Hustle"
> *Ninth Letter:* "The Corner," "Santayana, the Muralist," and "Trouble Man"
> *No Tell Motel:* "For the Good Times," "The Juju" (as "I Put a Spell On You"),
>   "The Prisoner's Wife," and "Round Midnight"
> *Ocho 15:* "The Poet Laureate"
> *Ploughshares:* "Sherman Ave. Love Poem"
> *Reverie:* "Ode to the Crossfader"
> *Tea Party:* "How to Split a Cold One"
> *Verse Wisconsin:* "November 26, 1980," "Practicing Fade-Aways," and "Song"

"Enter the Dragon," "Sherman Ave. Love Poem," and "Variation on a Theme By Eazy-E"
also appear in *Writing Self and Community: African American Poetry After the Civil Rights
Movement,* edited by Charles Henry Rowell. W.W. Norton, 2010.

Cover art: Krista Franklin
Author photo: Rachel Eliza Griffiths
Interior and cover design: Tom Helleberg

ISBN: 978-0-9819131-4-8

Cataloging-in-publication data available from the Library of Congress.

First edition: 2010

The publication of this book was made possible by grants from the
National Endowment for the Arts and the New York State Council of the Arts.

for Josie Grigsby,
my first teacher

What hurts
Is beautiful, the bruise
Of the lyric.

CONTENTS

FOREWORD

JOHN MURILLO IS DANGEROUS.

He is young and urban. He is African-American and Chicano. And he is male.

He fits the profile of dangerousness on multiple levels. He Drives While Black (*and* Brown). His Spanish surname, with its "ll" pronounced as "y," evokes the immigrant invasion so dear to television demagogues. He presents the specter of violence, either criminal or (worse) revolutionary, to the easily frightened majority.

Like most people who fit the profile, he is more endangered than dangerous, "more sinned against than sinning," as an English playwright put it centuries ago. The police have an unhealthy interest in the whereabouts of such persons, even in the "post-racial" era. President Obama may have won the Nobel Peace Prize, but, for some who walk the streets of this América, there is still no peace.

In fact, John Murillo is dangerous for all the wrong reasons. Murillo is a true poet, a wordsmith and a song-maker, intelligent, principled, compassionate and fearless. He speaks the truth in a lyrical language that provokes double takes of astonished recognition. He revels in his multiple identities without yielding to the clichés of identity politics or confirming the worst suspicions of the bigot brigade. He understands that poetry humanizes. He proves the proposition that the most "dangerous" and dehumanized among us are heartbreakingly human: tangible, tactile, fragile, mortal.

"Enter the Dragon" is Exhibit A. The poet, as a boy, goes to a movie with his father, cheers the Black martial-arts heroes on the screen, then watches in horror as his father is pulled over by the police on the way home:

When my father—this John Henry of a man—

Hides his hammer, doesn't buck, tucks away
His baritone, license and registration shaking as if

Showing a bathroom pass to a grade school
Principal, I learn the difference between cinema

And city, between the moviehouse cheers
Of old men and the silence that gets us home.

Here Murillo explores the tension between power and powerlessness, be-
tween the profile of dangerousness and the dangerous state, between the simu-
lated violence of popular culture and the everyday violence that maintains the
social order. That he does so in a narrative of wrenching vulnerability makes his
accomplishment all the more impressive.

Again and again, Murillo returns to that vulnerability, finding what is most
human in the most despised people and the most unforgiving circumstances. A
letter from his incarcerated poet-cousin reveals a moment of startling intimacy:

. . . He says he saw a man,
Convicted killer of six, bow his bald head,
Then raise his palms like a Muslim in prayer,
Catching rain like manna, his hands cupped
Now, and brought to his lips. Exactly three minutes
Before the guards called them in, my cousin
Says he watched this man's shoulders, back,
And, eventually, his entire body break into
Sobs, uncontrollable shudder, there on the yard
Where the other men watched—weightlifters and poets,
Prisoners and guards—until they couldn't anymore,
And turned their eyes to the ground . . .

Yet, Murillo does not strike the pose of a neglected prophet, stamping his cane
and shaking his finger in righteous indignation. He also points the finger at himself.
He knows when he has acted out the stereotypical role assigned to him, smashing his
own mirror image in a rage, reinforcing the borders and hierarchies of the damned.

In "Variation on a Theme by Eazy E," the poet begins with a stunning image:

Six cigarettes in the dark like the eyes of three jackals
Scattering bones and dust; the schoolboy musk
Of we who hadn't yet learned to wash properly—
This much I remember.

He also remembers that "lack of recognition was reason enough for all kinds/ Of mayhem. In other words, homeboy wasn't from around here." He calls himself the "Deacon in the church of this hallelujah beatdown," his "Knuckles fat and blue."

At other times, Murillo mocks his own adolescent machismo and gullibility. "Monster Boy," it seems, "Never came outside to play." His face was "inside out, string and pulp, vein and muscle meat, where skin should be." According to local legend, anyone could win three wishes by rubbing Monster Boy. One night, Murillo and his friends decided to test their courage.

. . . Alex, Eddie and I snuck out to find him. Alex's mom had just lost her job and needed money to make rent. Eddie wanted a dick as long as a turkey leg. And I needed Psycho Michael López out the way so Dolores Luna and I could fall in love.

Eddie volunteers to touch Monster Boy, then races past the other two— "crouched behind a Bonneville"—without ever telling them exactly what happened.

. . . but we suspected something when Alex's mom found work, Psycho Mike moved away, and Dolores spent the whole summer serenading Eddie.

The real courage here, of course, is the poet's courage to laugh at himself and the absurdity of a world that creates Monster Boys, instead of facing the real monsters.

Murillo's guiding spirit, "Virgil to my Dante," is prison poet Etheridge Knight. In "Flowers for Etheridge," Murillo makes a pilgrimage to Knight's grave in Indianapolis. Referring to Knight's famed poem about a rebellious inmate, "Hard Rock Returns to Prison from the Hospital for the Criminal Insane," Murillo movingly pays homage:

> . . . Maybe it wasn't Hard Rock at all, but you
> Who became our Destroyer, doer of what we dreamed done,
> Sayer of what we needed said. Etheridge, there are poets
> In prisons around the world reading by your fire. Poets
> For whom your words are sugar-tit, blanket, and roof.
>
> And not just bricked and barred in, but locked up in suits,
> Cubicles and kitchens. Men and women both, who know
> Too well the click of a closing door, cologne's last linger . . .

As Yusef Komunyakaa, himself a dangerous poet, points out, "Etheridge Knight was saved by poetry." So, too, was John Murillo. Now Murillo has become Knight's Destroyer, not "dangerous" in the stereotypical sense but very dangerous indeed, for he says "what we needed said." Now, with the publication of his first book, poets in prison—with or without bars—will read by John Murillo's fire. Leave the idea that "poetry makes nothing happen" to the poets whose poetry makes nothing happen. John Murillo will provide salvation to those who need poetry to save them.

And who among us does not need saving?

MARTÍN ESPADA
October, 2009

ODE TO THE CROSSFADER

Got this mixboard itch
        This bassline lifted
from my father's dusty
            wax   Forty crates stacked
in the back of the attic
        This static in the head-
phones   Hum in the blood
        This deep-bass buckshot
thump in the chest   Got
        reasons and seasons
pressed to both palms
        Two coins from each
realm   This memory
        Memory crossfaded and
cued   These knuckles'
        nicks and nightsweat
rites   This frantic
        abacus of scratch   Got
blood in the crates
        in the chest   in the dust
Field hollers to break-
        beats   My father's dusty

wax   My father's dust
      got reasons   Got night-
sweats and hollers
      pressed to both palms
breakbeats and hollers
      pressed to both palms
Static in the attic   Stacked
      crates of memory   Dust
blood and memory   Cross-
      faded and   Bass Cross-
faded and cued   Crossfaded
      and   Static   Stacked hollers
Got reasons in the dust
      in the chest   Got seasons
in the blood   In the head-
      phones' hum   This deep-
bass   buckshot   blood
      pressed   to both palms
My father's dust   pressed
      to both palms   Got
reasons and reasons
      and reasons

PRACTICING FADE-AWAYS

after Larry Levis

On a deserted playground in late day sun,
My palms dusted black, dribbling
A worn, leather ball behind my back, this loneliness
Echoes from the handball courts nearby.
Nearly all the markings—free throw lane, sideline,
Center circle—rubbed to nothing.
A crack in the earth cuts across the schoolyard,
Jagged as a scar on a choir boy's cheek.

Twenty years ago,
I ran this very court with nine other
Wanna-be ballers. We'd steal
Through peeled chain links, or hop
The gate, to get here: our blacktop Eden.
One boy, who had a funny pigeon-toed set shot
And a voice full of church bells, sang spirituals
Every time he made a basket,
The other boys humming along, laughing,
High-fives flying down the court.

And a boy we called 'The Sandman'
For how he put you to sleep with his shoulder fake or drop step,
Over six feet tall in the tenth grade,
Smooth talker with an itch for older guys' girlfriends.
One Sunday morning, they found him stabbed to death
Outside the Motel 6, pockets untouched,
Bills folded neatly against his beautiful cooling thigh.
And 'Downtown' Ricky Brown,
Whose family headed west when he was two,
But still called himself a New Yorker,
Who never pulled from less than thirty feet out,
And could bank shots blindfolded.
He went to Grambling, drove himself
Crazy with conspiracy theories and liquor,
Was last seen roaming the French Quarter, shoeless, babbling
About the Illuminati's six-hundred sixty-six ways
To enslave the populace.

At sixteen, I discovered
Venice Beach, with its thousand bodybuilders,
Roller skates, and red thong bikinis.
I would stand on the sidelines and watch
The local ballplayers, leaping and hollering
Quicksilver giants, run and gun,
Already grown into their man bodies,
Funkadelic rising from a boombox in the sand.
Now, all I hear are chain nets chiming as I sink
One fade-away after another,
The backboard, the pole, throwing a long shadow
Across the cracked black asphalt.

What the nets want must be this caress,
This stillness stretching
Along every avenue, over high school
Gymnasiums and deserted playgrounds,
And the ambulance drivers drifting into naps
Back at the station house.
What the boys who ran these courts wanted was
A lob pass high enough
To pull them into the sky,
Something they could catch in both hands
And hang from,
Long enough for someone to snap
A photograph, to hold them there,
Skybound. Risen.

THE CORNER

Hard rain and reggaeton score the night. On this block here,
At this hour, when even alley cats know to keep in shadow, backs
To the wall and ears piqued, the few renegade rain-soaked heads
You come across are here on business. Transactions and sales,
Give and take in the marketplace of the moon. If you wait
Long enough, they say, you can hear the hellhounds' bay. *The cross-*

Roads, in the swollen tongue of work-weary bluesmen across
Geography and generations. Hoodoo Land. 'Legba's turf. It's here,
They say, where Robert Johnson sold his soul to learn the sweet
Secret of conjuring moonlight from string and wood. When back-
Roads all seemed to lead to the same place, men fresh from their cells
Came to strike deals on a new start in life, to get ahead.

Take this young boy, JoJo. Fresh out the joint, before he'd head
Anywhere near his mama's house, he'd run straight here. Across
The street from the carryout and check cashing spot, he'll peddle
His rocks to anybody who pushes past. Even little Ebony. Hear
She was almost prom queen, drove the young boys crazy back
In the days before JoJo got hold of her. How the weight

Melts from face and neck. How skin cankers, and blood and sweat
Crust corners of lips licked only in wet dreams. How she gives head
Now by the dumpster behind the church, fucks, how fast five bucks
Find their way back to JoJo's hands. And Jesus, on a stone cross,
Watches it all from on high. How it begins, ends, and begins again here.
On the corner. Tonight, rain clouds bruise the sky. JoJo sells

Like a man with plans, as if he can buy his way away. Sells
As if he were the first to have such ideas. As if *moving weight*
Wasn't just a new name for an old dream. When his mama was out here,
They called it *pushing*. By the time his daughter's head
Can fit the first pink wig, they'll be calling it something else. The cross-
Roads has seen it all. Seven hundred sixty-two JoJos , JoJoing back

To the days of fire-can crooners, doo-wop daddies and off-key back-
Up singers, warming hands and running from the 'rollers. As if their cells
Were hardwired for trouble, they'd find new lines to cross and cross
Again. And find themselves back on the courtyard, lifting weights.
Or back on cots, crumpling "Dear John" letters, slipping heads
In and out of nooses. After years locked down, they all end up back here.

Maybe you've seen how they come back—years lifting or losing weight,
Thugs turned saint or cell-block Muslim, some with heads
Full of cross-the-system schemes, some half-dead. Always, always, here.

HUSTLE

"Thinkin' of a master plan,
cuz ain't nothin' but sweat inside my hand."
—*Rakim*

Got drive enough to grab the moon with these hands,
These hard working, snatch-opportunity hands.

Left Soledad broke, made my first thirty G's—
That was September, now it's June—with these hands.

I serve Mama for free, keep her off these streets,
Off her knees, out of motel rooms, with these hands.

My baby girl asked me, *Daddy, what's 'turn tricks'?*
Got to pull us up out of here soon with these hands.

A man ain't a man if he can't feed himself.
I'm carving *steaks* each afternoon with these hands!

I hear minimum wage is about six bucks.
Fuck I look like pushing a broom with these hands?

Read a book in my cell, said I was the one
Built pyramids, temples, and tombs. (With *these* hands?)

At ten, I was a lookout. Then learned to bag,
How to cook up rocks in a spoon with these hands.

Lost a good woman, said the life was too much.
Some nights I still smell her perfume on these hands.

No way to know, but maybe Daddy sang blues.
Blood explains the itch of his tune in these hands.

AT THE METRO

An old man's upturned palm;
Red clay cracking under passing clouds.

SANTAYANA, THE MURALIST

Outside Chong's liquor store, you'll meet a man
Spraying corridos along a façade. He carries the soul
Of la raza in his cans, he claims. Hopes to change
The world one wall at a time. His bold blues,
Greens, and golds bring to mind the photos you pore
Over in *National Geographic*. Paint caps

Dot the sidewalk like spilled Skittles. His Dodgers cap
Tilts to one side, more pachuco than painter. This man
Aerosols Aztlan across barrio brick for all the poor
To see: Aztec warriors, old Mexican washwomen, dios del sol.
See his lowriders and zoot suiters battle badges and blue
Uniforms. "¿Sabes qué, hombre? Things don't change

Much around here. Haven't really changed
Since Roosevelt and his American concentration camps."
He fingers the pump on a can of crimson. "Blew
Me away when I read about that shit. The white man
Points at Hitler and calls *him* evil? Please! *His* soul
Should burn the way he locked up them Japanese." A poorly

Dressed elderly man walks over. Santayana pours
A fistful of nickels into his dingy fedora. Fingers more change
In his other pocket. Gives that away too. The sole
Heir to the Rivera legacy—let him tell it—keeps
A buck knife close as skin, but still believes that man's
True nature, "beneath the grime," is gold. His blue

Sputters. Coughs. Falls from his hand. "This blue
Is the hardest of all to match. With aerosol, you can't pour
And blend like the ancients did with plants and clays. Nowadays a man
Gotta mix while he sprays. But that could change
The whole piece. ¿Tú sabes? And the cap
Don't really tell what's inside the can. Kinda like the soul,
¿Qué no? You can look beautiful on the outside and your soul

Be all fucked up on the inside. How blood drips red, but is blue
In your veins? Can't tell shit from the outside, man." His cap
Tilted back, a faded gang tattoo wipes a sweaty brow. He pours
A forty down his throat, stares down the sun. "Yep, change
Gonna have to come. Or we all gonna be like that old man.

Not only in his pocket, but in his soul, he's poor.
Singing the blues, in fact. But check it: Begging change,
You think the man just means the coins in his cap?"

SHERMAN AVE. LOVE POEM

A street sweeper rounds
    the corner, headlights
stretching a man's silhouette
    across the cool brick
of a brownstone. A window
    rattles, creaks, lifts open
from his rib, and a woman
    steps through, pushes

off the ledge. Doesn't flail,
    doesn't scream, or scratch
at passing brick. Mid-flight,
    she lies flat, spreads her
swollen shadow onto
    a fire hydrant. She is sure

as gravity. The man
    crossing the street, all rib
and open eye, clutches
    his Koran. Read in prison
how pregnant women
    would dive from slave ships.
Thought then, and believes
    Now more than ever: this is
the one true act.

ENTER THE DRAGON

Los Angeles, California, 1976

For me, the movie starts with a black man
Leaping into an orbit of badges, tiny moons

Catching the sheen of his perfect black afro.
Arc kicks, karate chops, and thirty cops

On their backs. It starts with the swagger,
The cool lean into the leather front seat

Of the black and white he takes off in.
Deep hallelujahs of moviegoers drown

Out the *wah wah* guitar. Salt & butter
High-fives, *Right on, brother!* and Daddy

Glowing so bright he can light the screen
All by himself. This is how it goes down.

Friday night and my father drives us
Home from the late show, two heroes

Cadillacking across King Boulevard.
In the car's dark cab, we jab and clutch,

Jim Kelly and Bruce Lee with popcorn
Breath, and almost miss the lights flashing

In the cracked side mirror. I know what's
Under the seat, but when the uniforms

Approach from the rear quarter panel,
When the fat one leans so far into my father's

Window I can smell his long day's work,
When my father—this John Henry of a man—

Hides his hammer, doesn't buck, tucks away
His baritone, license and registration shaking as if

Showing a bathroom pass to a grade school
Principal, I learn the difference between cinema

And city, between the moviehouse cheers
Of old men and the silence that gets us home.

1989

There are no windows here, and the walls
Are lined with egg cartons. So if we listen
Past the sampled piano, drum kick
And speakerbox rumble, we'd still not hear
The robins celebrating daybreak.
The engineer worries the mixboard,
Something about a hiss lurking between notes.
Dollar Bill curses the engineer, time
We don't have. Says it's just a demo
And doesn't need perfecting. "Niggas
Always want to make like Quincy Jones
When you're paying by the hour."
Deejay Eddie Scizzorhandz—because he cuts
So nice—taps ashes into an empty pizza box,
Head nodding to his latest masterpiece:
Beethoven spliced with Mingus,
Mixed with Frankie Beverly, all laid
On Billy Squire's "Big Beat."
I'm in a corner, crossing out and rewriting
Lines I'll want to forget years later,

Looking up every now and then,
To watch Sheik Spear, Pomona's finest emcee,
In the vocal booth, spitting rhymes
He never bothers putting to paper,
Nearly hypnotized by the gold-plated cross
Swinging from his neck as he, too,
Will swing, days from now, before
They cut him from the rafters of a jail cell.

RENEGADES OF FUNK

for Patrick Rosal

I

When we were twelve, we taught ourselves to fly,
To tuck the sky beneath our feet, to spin
The world on fingertips. To pirouette
On elbows, heads, and backs, to run away
While standing still. So when Miss Jefferson—
Her eyebrows shaved then painted black, the spot
Of lipstick on her one good tooth—would praise
The genius Newton, I knew then to keep
Her close, to trust her like a chicken hawk
At Colonel Sanders'. *I refute your laws,*
Oppressor! I'm the truth you cannot stop!
Busting headspins on her desk, a moonwalk
Out the door. Referred to Mr. Brown's
Detention. *All them try'na keep us down!*

II

Attention: Rhythm's why they keep us. Down
    In Memphis, bluesmen beg the sky to pour
Down liquor. Empty bottles, barren hands.
    A pawn shop banjo gathers dust. Guitars
Sit idle, songs forgotten. Ghosts come late
    To find the crossroads cluttered, strip malls now

Where haints once hung. The young, it seems, forget
        The drum and how it bled, the dream and how
It fed the mothers on the auction block.
        But rhythm's why they keep us. Rhythm's why
We've kept up. Cotton fields and backs
        That creak, a song for every lash, a cry
On beat, and blues sucked dry. The strip malls bleed
        The ghosts from banjos. Hollers caught in greed.

III   The ghosts. The angels. Holocausts. The need
To shake these shackles, field songs in our bones.
As if, at twelve, we knew all this, we named
Our best moves *free*: to *break* and *pop-lock*, blood
And bruises marking rites. We'd gather, dance
Ourselves electric, stomp and conjure storm,
Old lightning in our limbs. We thunderstruck
Maroons, machete wielding silhouettes,
Reject the fetters, come together still—
Some call it *Capoeira*, call it *street-
Dance*. We say *culture*. Say *survival*.
Bahia's berimbau or Boombox in
The "Boogie Down": a killing art as play,
An ancient killing art to break us free.

IV   *O Lord, send somethin' down to break us free,*
Said send us somethin' now to set us free.
Swing low Your chariot to rescue we.
The calls went up in every blessed field.
The people shouting, singing in the fields.
They lit the torches, compromised the yield.
This earthly house is gonna soon decay,
Said look like Massa's house gon' soon decay.
I got my castle. Where he plan to stay?
Some waited in the hills till nightfall came,
An exodus of thousands. When night came,
They built their fires, sang into the flames:
Upon the mountaintop, the Good Lord spoke.
And out His mouth came the fire and the smoke.

V   The art of spitting fire? How to smoke
A fool without a gun? We learned that too.
We studied master poets—Kane, not Keats;
Rakim, not Rilke. "Raw," "I Ain't No Joke,"
Our Nightingales and Orpheus. And few
There were among us couldn't ride a beat
In strict tetrameter. Impromptu odes
And elegies—instead of slanting rhymes

We *gangster lean*ed them, kicking seventeen
Entendre couplets just to fuck with old
Miss Jefferson, the Newton freak. Sometimes
We even got her out her seat, her ten
Thin digits waving side to side, held high
And hiding nothing. Where our eyes could see.

VI   And we knew nothing but what eyes could see—
The burnt-out liquor stores and beauty shops,
Mechanics' lots, abandoned, boarded up
Pastrami shacks where, seemed like everyday,
We used to ditch class, battle Centipedes
And Space Invaders. Gone. Or going fast.
What eyes could see was flux—the world, and us,
And all we knew, like smoke. So renegade
We did, against erasure, time, and, hell,
We thought, against the Reaper, too. We left
Our names in citadels, sprayed hieroglyphs
In church. Our rebel yells in aerosol—
We bomb therefore we are. We break therefore
We are. We spit the gospel. Therefore, Are.

VII   The walls are sprayed in gospel: This is for
The ones who never made the magazines.
    Between breakbeats and bad breaks, broken homes
And flat broke, caught but never crushed. The stars
    We knew we were, who recognized the shine
Despite the shade. We renegade in rhyme,
    In dance, on trains and walls. We renegade
In lecture halls, the *yes, yes, y'all's* in suits,
    Construction boots, and aprons. Out of work
Or nine to five, still renegade. Those laid
    To rest, forgotten renegades, in dirt
Too soon with Kuriaki, Pun, and Pac—
    I sing your names in praise, remember why
When we were twelve, we taught ourselves to fly.

UP JUMP THE BOOGIE, OR GEORGE CLINTON COUNSELS THE CREATIVE WRITING STUDENT

for Hafizah and Olivia

You say they trigonometry life
    brain when they need bone
        Try to scrape the cool
from the womb of you

    You say they junk your funk
        De-pimp your limp
Hush the boom-clack
    at the base of your back

Say they hate the words wet
    'cause they never learned to swim

      Don't mute the moon's
    blue vocabulary
Need to know
    the need   To know is secondary

Up jump the boogie   See the beauty you be
    and dance even when
        you the only music

THE POET LAUREATE

Pushed a wide-bodied Bonneville
Up and down Exposition Boulevard,
Dirty dice swinging from the mirror
When he bent corners, deep leaning
Into leather, half-pint of Jack in his lap.
Left youngbloods scratching heads,
Watching perfumed hips saunter onto
His porch, a different creak each week.

Neighbors say he did a bid for bank
Robbing, cash stashed to keep rent
Steady. Neighbors say he was a hoodoo
Man from Louisiana, run up west
By a married man's Remington. Ask
Me and I'll talk about chocolate,
A door to door sale, knock-kneed steps
Up a strange man's stoop. Ask me,

I'll tell you about a busted screen door,
A chipped tooth grin, swigs of gin
From a mayonnaise jar; how, bloated
And bloodshot, he caught me peeking
Around his waist at his walls of books, his
Stacks of books, furniture made of books,
Offered to buy my whole box if I'd stay
To hear some poems he wrote.

Ask about that day and I'll tell you
About the ghost of good sense,
A latch's click, and a Smith-Corona
Glowing on a milk crate. I'll tell you
About the keys' cold contours, the reams
By the door, and thirty years learning
What he must have meant, laughing:
Youngblood, you done fucked up good.

MONSTER BOY

Never came outside to play. Never left his yard except to empty his mother's trash, and even then, just after midnight, as if the neighborhood slept. They said his face was born inside out, string and pulp, vein and muscle meat, where skin should be. They said it was bad luck to look at him but good to grab him. They said if you could rub his head—or better, his belly—you could win three wishes. But if you stared into his eyes for more than two seconds, you'd suffer a week's worth of dysentery, would lose all the hair on your privates, and your pinga would shrivel to Minute Rice. One night, when nothing was on TV, Alex, Eddie, and I snuck out to find him. Alex's mom had just lost her job and needed money to make rent. Eddie wanted a dick as long as a turkey leg. And I needed Psycho Michael López out the way so Dolores Luna and I could fall in love. The moon hung high and round as one of Dolores' breasts. Steady Eddie hopped the back fence while Alex and I crouched behind a Bonneville. He stayed gone a good five minutes before sprinting past us, panting, "I'll tell you about it later!" Later, he told us nothing, but we suspected something when Alex's mom found work, Psycho Mike moved away, and Dolores spent that whole summer serenading Eddie.

VARIATION ON A THEME BY EAZY E

Six cigarettes in the dark like the eyes of three jackals
Scattering bones and dust; the schoolboy musk
Of we who hadn't yet learned to wash properly—
This much I remember. And I can still taste that summer,
The blood of it, when a certain breeze blows.
Through a screen door, someone's television plays
The theme song from *S.W.A.T.* When Jojo gives the signal,
Every dog on St. Andrews Place stirs to alarm.
I'm told predators abhor violence, are pacifists at heart.
Truth is, there was not a pacifist among us.
Fifteen year olds are violent by nature. Even the love
We dreamed of then—all thrust and sweat, tussle and scratch—
Smells of the kill. Of course, the jack move is no exception.
And lack of recognition is reason enough for all kinds
Of mayhem. In other words, homeboy wasn't from around here.
Hey, Homey! Don't I know you from somewhere?
Let me talk to you real quick! Begins the chase, the catch
The coldest night in August, the sharpened spoon
Of logic lodged midway between sternum and clavicle.
And when we look toward the sky, even the moon
Holds its breath, goes still, and prays. That was the night
I gave birth to myself: Big Slim, the Chuck Taylor Shogun,

Deacon in the church of this hallelujah beatdown.
The moon gasps, and we slam the car doors, peel
Into the night. When Jojo passes me the spliff, I try to still my fingers,
Knuckles fat and blue, spilling ashes on the gearbox.
He pops a tape in, twists the volume high as it will go.
The woofers rattle our ribcages, teeth,
The windows, the rearview.

NOVEMBER 26, 1980

Five faces bunched in the glow of an old
Floor model black and white, and a shadow
The shape of knuckles splashed
Against the living room wall, my father
Hollers when *Hands of Stone*, Roberto Durán,
Waves off the fight and slinks
Toward the corner, cut-man and handlers
Struck dumb as ringside tuxes, dumb
As the uncles and cousins squeezed
Onto our couch, cigarettes hanging from every open mouth.
Sugar Ray, all rhythm and blur, afro and short shorts, deals
A three-piece to the gut for good measure,
And Durán is done. Uncle Buck
Praises Jesus, c-note riding on Ray in eight. Says
He's late for a cross-town *Rhonda rendezvous*,
Grinding the air, smacking imaginary ass.

Cash in his pocket, a woman to see, we know
Buck won't be with us for a good few days.
What we don't know is why. What we can't know
Is how Rhonda—the one he won't bring by
Since Crazy Pete caught her peeking
At his cards and ran home to load his Roscoe,
She of the Chaka Khan wigs and thick lips—hip
To Buck's heavy betting and the bragged-on odds,
Smells presidents from miles away, the fresh bulge
Of an old billfold, and is telephoning homeboys
From the other side of Exposition Boulevard.
Buck grabs his coat, shuffling into night.

We don't know the next time we'll see Buck
Is in traction—bandaged, jaw wired shut,
Tubes for piss and shit. Back home,
I'll be in charge of soup and vitamin shakes,
The spoons he'll push away, the straws he'll spit out.
I'll say nothing of the whispers, the rumors
That he's marked as a mark now. I'll not repeat
That a pussy-whipped gambler ain't too long
For this world. I'll leave the grown-up talk
To grown-ups. Make the shakes, serve the soup.

At nine, I've years to know a thing about this
Kind of pain, the kind with little to do
With bicycle chains, aluminum bats, boots
Between shoulder blades. But I know enough
Not to refuse this man his bottle of Night Train.
When he motions for it, I know I'm not supposed to, but
I'll unscrew the top, put it to his lips, watch the burn—
The stitches' give, scabs scratched open
In what passes for sleep—and halfway understand,
Watching Buck flip channels, every one
Replaying that last long round, the night,
The first clear words we've heard from Uncle Buck
Since he left us for his rendezvous:
No más, no más, no más.

DREAM FRAGMENT WITH
A SHOT CLOCK AND WHISTLES IN IT

It starts with an asphalt sky
   blacktop courts buzzards

perched on every rusted rim
   It always starts here I'm

bringing the ball up left-
   handed just like you

left-handed just like you
   taught me cross half court

stutter step reverse pivot
   and pull *point your elbow*

at the bucket boy and follow
   through always follow

through got to get up gather
   my legs lift lock into

eyes eager to peck the brittle
   bones of my lay ups shot-

clock dies a whistle blows
   Out of bounds ball in hand

scan the court for an open
            man   *daddy did you hear*

the Lakers got Shaquille
            think this'll be our season

eyes eager to peck the brittle
            brittle bones of my lay ups

nowhere to pass   a whistle
            blows   *boy my lungs are*

black as basketball grooves
            It ain't no more seasons

and I begin again   Pushing
            upcourt   Blacktop Sisyphus

in sweatsocks   Can't see
            the clock but I know it's

there   Can't see the clock
            but I know it's there

It ain't no more seasons
            Just a few quick ticks

and that rock you squeezin
    stutter step   another whistle

and I am five again   synthetic
    leather in hand   You hold me

overhead   laugh   *now we both*
    got some sun to hold onto

Under skies as cracked and
    lovely as this concrete

that keeps us from falling
    I push the ball off fingertips

and listen for the kiss of
    chain nets like a glass cage

chain nets like a glass cage
    shattered on a planet far away

HOW TO SPLIT A COLD ONE

Olvera Street, Los Angeles, CA

Mira los zopilotes, my uncle Beto tells me.
Everywhere you look, vultures.
His voice cuts through camera shutters
And the shuffle of Birkenstocks,
Across counters covered by Mexican flags,
Maracas, and mariachi figurines.
I betchu these gabachos think Pancho Villa
Is a conga player from East L.A.,
And La Raza is something you shave with.
A blond boy in a Speedy González tank top
Snaps a shot of my uncle's middle finger.

When I was last here, I was the boy's age.
Those were the days Uncle Beto refused
To speak Spanish, blasted Pat Benatar
From Camaro tweeters, and wore blonde hairs
Splayed across his varsity letter
Like soldier's brass. I hold my laugh
Long enough to pay for a Zapatista t-shirt
And a Jimmy Baca paperback when he takes me
Back to my own high school days:
High top fades, flip up shades,

And leather Back to Africa medallions.
Jokes about the week I changed my name
To *Juanito X*, and stopped eating chorizo.
Oh, so now you're ready to be Mexican?
The silence hangs heavy between us
Like the t-shirts flanking the cashier,
A slogan slung across the chest
Like a bandolier: *DRINK CULTURA!*

Last time we were here, my afro
Was as big as my body. My grandmother
Bought a clay jar like the one shattered
By a Texas cop's buckshot
When she first came up from *Aguascalientes*.
When we got home, she filled it
With cool water and offered me a sip.
I tipped the jug, grains of sand
Swimming across the crooked borders
Of my teeth, and spat across the kitchen floor.
That's the earth you taste, M'ijo. The land
we come from. It's good for you.
Now drink.

Beto and I step out into the sun. Dry.
Thirsty. A west wind brings us a tray
Of carne asada, the kind Grandma used to make
On Saturdays just like this. The kind
Grandpa taught me to wash down
With tall bottles of Corona. Without words,
We walk over, seat ourselves, and
Hard-think drink orders. Without words,
We face each other, reading the menus. Words
Like *Corona* and *Cultura*
Simmering in closed mouths.

SIN VERGÜENZA

para Valéria

The years spread between us like the black
Between stars. My cousin and me in a Chicago bar,
Meeting for the first time in fifteen years, business
Travel doing the work blood hasn't been able to.
Though she doesn't believe me when I tell her,
She looks the same now as she did as a teen.
She tugs at my graying beard, rubs my bald head,
Says I've gotten old.

When she was a toddler, I fed my cousin fish sticks,
French fries, red Kool-Aid with too much sugar.
I would read to her from oversized picture books
Stories where the pretty princess always
Endured the witch, children escaped,
The line between good and wicked straight as a wand.
Now I buy her booze. Lots of it.
We start a tab, grab a corner table. Realize
We now have, between us, one dead grandfather,
Two dead fathers—cancer claiming one, cirrhosis the other,
Alcoholics both—two bruised mothers
Who no longer speak, and for each of us, a fistful
Of missteps and missed steps.
We sit and drink, *sin vergüenza*, without shame,
Showing each other scars, some fresh, some familiar,
Every one our own.

If we were a storybook, I would read us
Aloud, let the world wonder how it is
In these stories, the damsels become dragons, apples
Swallow villages, and kings sprout horns. I would
Read us loudly, *sin vergüenza*, because shame
Is a luxury lost on the wretched—battle weary
Dragonslayers, knights who know to count each survival,
Every arrow that pierced and poisoned but did not kill,
All the falls, the hatchets and the hexes,
Count survivals and call them blessings.

Cousin, though you have been damsel, tonight
You, too, are dragon—relentless fire, insistent breath,
Bidding me—*remember, remember, remember.*
Sin vergüenza, you tell me what you remember
Of the houses where you nightmared, the midnight
Scent of honeysuckle, baby powder, blood.
You tell me without shame, and I am almost ashamed
To tell you how fifteen years ago I ran away
To find my own dragons, castles, a damsel needing rescue.
How it has taken me each season and every mile walked
To arrive at this table here tonight, to drink from this very glass,
To learn, after all, that my castle was fantasy, damsel memory,
And dragon was a place called home. We touch glasses
And you tell me in other tongues, ways you've learned

To say *salute*. But for the shaken ice, the clinking rims
Sound like the storybook signal to turn the page.

I tell this story *sin vergüenza*. Me and my baby cousin
In a Bucktown bar, throwing back glasses of Grey Goose,
Hennessey, Bacardi. We drop quarters into the slots
Of a pool table, snatch cues off the rack like battle axes.
We laugh at the aches our bodies have become—
Girl cousin circling the table on a bum left foot,
Boy cousin's crackling scapula, bones creaking across the green.
It's nearly three o'clock in the morning, which is to say
The place is empty except for some locals
Chatting up the bartender, the anchorman on TV
Mouthing wars and wars to come. Outside,
The leaves curl into themselves like the old man
Sleeping in the doorjamb, an overcoat
Wrapping him against the wind, because, after all,
It is October, and this is Chicago. We are far
Past drunk. Family, circling the table, each other.
Someone's stolen the triangle so we gather stripes,
Solids, by hand. One of us watching
While the other one breaks.

TROUBLE MAN

It's the bone of a question
    Caught in your throat,
Pre-dawn sighs of the day's
    First traffic, shoulders like
Fists under your skin. Say
    It's raining this morning,
You've just left a woman's
    Blue musk and duvet,
To find devil knows what
    In the world, your wet collar,
Too thin jacket, no match
    For pissed off sky gods.
And say this car pulls near,
    Plastic bag for passenger
Side window, trading rain
    For music. Marvin Gaye.
And maybe you know
    This song. How long
Since a man you called father
    Troubled the hi-fi, smoldering
Newport in hand, and ran
    This record under a needle.

How long since a man's
　　Broken falsetto colored
Every hour indigo. Years
　　Since he drifted, dreaming
Into rice fields, stammered
　　Cracked Vietcong, gunboats
And helicopters swirling
　　In his head. Years since
His own long walks, silent
　　Returns, and Marvin's
Many voices his only salve.
　　He came up harder than
You know, your father.
　　Didn't make it by the rules.
Your father came up hard,
　　Didn't get to make no rules.
Graying beard, callused hands,
　　Fingernails thick as nickels,
You were the boy who became
　　That man, without meaning

To, and know now: A man's
    Life is never measured
In beats, but beat-downs,
    Not line breaks, just breaks.
You hear Marvin fade down
    The avenue and it caresses you
Like a brick: Your father,
    Marvin, and men like them,
Have already moaned every
    Book you will ever write.
This you know, baby. This
    You know.

FLOWERS FOR ETHERIDGE

Crown Hill Cemetery, Indianapolis, IN

I'm spending half this afternoon apologizing to ghosts,
Stepping over gravestones, the poet's *Belly Song*
In one hand, a ten dollar bouquet in the other.

Half the afternoon hanging with housewives
And murderers, aristocrats and paupers, searching
For the poet whose name is writ in the blood

Of soothsayers, shapeshifters, and slaves; poet
Who gave us Hard Rock, Shine, and Freckle-Faced
Gerald. Scanning tombstones, browsing epitaphs

Of complete strangers—daughters and uncles,
Grandmothers and husbands—just eleven miles
From where my father last breathed; this overcast,

Underwhelming, graveyard traipsing day, searching
For the poet, Virgil to my Dante, who will whisper
The poem that says all I need said, will ever need to say.

|| The poet, Levis, speaks of places where the eye can starve.
I say there are places, also, where the ear learns famine—

The silences so absolute, the pauses between words
Lasting longer than what we mean to say. My father

Has no gravesite, his dying wish to be cremated,
Scattered in the Pacific, half carried out. He knew

These silences well, though in life was anything but.
He never read much, but I imagine would have loved

You, Etheridge, your smoke-tinged toasts, the gospel

Of the getting by, the left behind and fucked up. Strong
Sips in the bar's blackest corner, smoke rings and blues.

He wrote me once, my father. From his deathbed.
Not poetry, but a letter. It starts like this: *I'm sorry*

If you can't read this. My hands are not writing
So well. As if his hands were not his hands,

But two grown men with their own comings and goings,
Workers who, out of handicap or lethargy, stopped
Doing the job they were hired to do. Agent Orange

Ate his lungs, and chemo took care of the rest. But
First, he needed to say what needed saying. *I'm sorry...*

My hands are not writing so well. Hands that have
Held both grandbabies and grenades, stumble under
The weight of a number two pencil. Imagine—three
Grams of wood and lead, load enough to break a man.

My cousin is a poet, Etheridge, like us. He writes
Letters from the same prison you served in. Maybe,
Even the same cell, the very cot where you wrote
Of ancestry. His letters come faster than I can answer.

One day soon, for no good reason,
I'll stop writing back altogether.

.

In one letter, he reminds me of a summer thirty years back,
The two of us pulled to the curb for riding double on a bike,
Questioned as if caught with a grown woman's pocketbook,

My cousin asking the officer if he'd haul us to *Juvey*.
Me asking my cousin what the hell was a *Juvey*,

The day he learned how easy to hate cops,
The day I vowed never again to get caught.

My cousin, the poet, takes correspondence courses
From Ball State, is working hard toward his bachelor's.
He sends me stories, poems, and papers he writes for classes,

Keeps me up to date
On prison yard seminars,
Forums and debates—

Who really runs America, what the Bildebergs plan,
When the New World Order first kicked in—

Says he's reading long after the block goes dark,
Fanon, Van Sertima, and John Henrik Clarke,

Drops a new gem each time he writes.

.

He's up for appeal at the end of the month. I think he's guilty
Of being in the wrong place and time. In the wrong skin
And day. He's guilty in time and skin. Place pending.

IV It's a poet's simple duty to make pilgrimage. To lay
Flowers on the graves of other poets. Levis,
When in Rome, stopped by to see Keats, his name

On a nearby gravestone, his own inscripted only:
Here lies one whose name is writ in water. Water's
What brung us here. Water's what swallowed

The bones sucked by the sharks that followed
The boats; when pregnant women leapt instead
Of staying the journey. Mbembe jumped and you

Were shattered. But maybe he knew something
Of water's legacy. Ghosts in the sewers, cold running
Tap. Pooled memory. Ancestry more than idea.

Etheridge, your name is writ in water. Water
And blood. Blood and stone. Stone you can see
Through, stone like water. How many bones

Beneath the blue? How many fathoms below? How
To fathom, Etheridge, just how deep it can go?
We read about the needles, belts, the sliding back

And half-kicked habits. Maybe you knew something
Ancestral, too, beyond photographs taped to your wall.
Maybe you saw through stone. Fathomed abyss.

V I was in Rome a few months back. Day trip by train,
Down from Milan and up again. Caught up in a workers'

Rally at the ruins, a thousand thousand red t-shirts,
Banners and baseball caps chanting down empire.

I wanted to see Keats, but never made it over. I wondered,
Aside from battle, if you had ever made it this far. I know

My cousin hasn't. My father may have, on his way
Somewhere else, in fatigues most likely, boots shined

And spit polished. He was a soldier in a different war,
He was a casualty of the same war. Nam, Korea, Mississippi,

Compton. Crosshaired and lit. Legions out of work workers,
Marching and fallen, silent or praying, whether or not

They believe in any god, these faces at the Roman ruins
Knew something of this despair, the need to leap.

They chanted and sang, knowing no walls would tumble.
Not poetry, exactly, just something what needed saying.

VI There was a day on the yard, my cousin writes,
When, between sets, it began to sprinkle. Rain
Dotted the benches, beaded on gravel and iron.
Biceps, tattooed and taut, flinched, then welcomed
This unexpected caress. He says he saw a man,
Convicted killer of six, bow his bald head,
Then raise his palms like a Muslim in prayer,
Catching rain like manna, his hands cupped
Now, and brought to his lips. Exactly three minutes
Before the guards called them in, my cousin
Says he watched this man's shoulders, back,
And eventually, his entire body break into
Sobs, uncontrollable shudder, there on the yard
Where the other men watched—weightlifters and poets,
Prisoners and guards—until they couldn't anymore,
And turned their eyes to the ground. Rain worked
Its way between bars and plates, into dirt, into
Every porous stone. Pushing, pushing.

VII Your song, your chanting, shook no chains, crumbled no walls,
Or snatched so much as a minute from any man's calendar.

Maybe that's not the way our work works. Maybe it's enough
Just to say words like "ancestry," "father," "mother," "niece."

Maybe it's enough to stand upright, grab your cock and scream—
To tell the world, a man's standing here. I don't know,

But something brung me, Etheridge. Something more
Than water. Maybe it wasn't Hard Rock at all, but you,

Who became our Destroyer, doer of what we dreamed done,
Sayer of what we needed said. Etheridge, there are poets

In prisons around the world reading by your fire. Poets
For whom your words are sugar-tit, blanket, and roof.

And not just bricked and barred in, but locked up in suits,
Cubicles and kitchens. Men and women both, who know

Too well the click of a closing door, cologne's last linger,
The knowledge that love done got up and gone. Done split

With all your best shit. May be enough to know another strutted
Straight through the pain. Pimp-walked this road, and will again.

VIII Indiana. Hoosier State. Home of the buzzer
Beater, Larry Bird and Oscar Robertson.
Courts my father learned to back down
Men twice his size, all the way down
Beneath the bucket and hook, trucks flying
Flags of confederate design. Hoosier State,
Home of the first and last burning cross
I've ever seen, the fall and rise of Ku Klux
And other clans, black men gutted,
Strung up and skinned, Bobby Knight
Slapping a two guard across the face.
Hoosier Dome, home to whites only
Ball clubs and balconies, no nigger heaven,
Presbyterian beatdown, broke bottle
And barroom tussle, muscled men
Backed down, way down. Gutbucket
Ghost stories. My father backing men
Down and those who didn't got Bobby
Knighted. On backroads, ball courts,

And barrooms, beat like buzzers.
Hoosier State, home of the poet,
Shrapnel-pierced and spook-ridden,
Mississippi to Marion County. Home
To my Hoosier Daddy, known
To knife men twice his size, legend
That Crown Hill hosts at least a dozen
Of his eviscerated bloods. Buckets
Of hard liquor licked from lips
Of street walking Hoosier mamas,
Backroad Sallies, sometimes twice
His size. Black skinned Hoosier
Two guard, never backed down, never tried,
But trucked to fly flags, strung up
And shot at. Purple-starred Hoosier soldier,
Come home decorated, still
No heaven for a ball playing nigger.

IX *I'm sorry if you can't read this.*
My hands are not writing so well.

X And was there a bus ride, maybe, when my father dropped
Onto the seat next to you, you staring out the window
(Being a poet), my father striking up conversation (being

My father), you preoccupied with a missing measure
Or a not-quite-broken-right line, polite at first, but tuning
Him out, the way I would, when as a teen, I discovered

The magic of a well-written love letter, metaphor before
I had a word for it, the reason behind the ballads rising
From old men's radios, and my father talking on through

My indifference, my well-timed "yeah's" and "mm-hmm's,"
Like you, trying to catch the wing of an idea slamming
Against the pane then gone forever out the open window,

My father talking right through it and you, with a good six miles
Of potholes and pissy seats to go, figure what the hell,
Turn to face my father, eight years your junior, to listen

To his rants about crackers and taxes, fixed elections, niggers
Not like they used to be, and did he bum a cigarette from you,
Or you from him, and did you laugh at the story he loves

About a night in Biloxi, and how many people—there
Or here—did you find in common, talking loud shit,
Other passengers shooting looks but knowing better

Than to glare too long, sensing consequence in the veterans'
Thousand yard stares, and did you double him over, my father,
With a toast about Shine and the Titanic, laughing, howling,

Rot-toothed and raucous, then almost miss your stop, stunned
Mute when you brought up Pyongyang, Saigon, napalmed skies,
And did you share that bone-heavy hush for the rest of the ride?

XI I've seen photos of Keats' grave, headstone reaching
For heaven, crowded with chrysanthemums and lilies,
Memorial polished by fingers and kisses, poet hopefuls
And dedicated readers. Tourists. A thousand daily visits.

You have no headstone. No signs point to your plot,
The grass surrounding your grave, fresh, free of prints.
Not a single soft petal to freshen the air above you.
No flowers, no frills— "Poet. Son. Father. Brother."

Here are the roses and baby's breath, the waxflowers
Laid at your stone. Here is the letter I meant to write
Years ago, and bring to lay here too. Here is my father's
Baritone, bursting from my own two lungs, a belly song

Sung too late. Here is a hand held out to you, Etheridge,
Poet to poet, man to exhausted man. Here is a day
Set aside for communion, ancestry transcending blood.
Here is my blood. Here is my history stretching for acres.

Here is half my family buried, a breeze through willows
In summer. Here is summer. Here is the sun crouching
Behind a mausoleum, my shadow crossing your grave. Here
Are the flowers laid on the poem chiseled into your stone.

XII WE FREE SINGERS BE. Four easy words
Cut into your flatstone, chanted over the car radio
As I back out of Crown Hill, out of Indiana, out
Of a past I never knew as my own. What I mean
Is something between recovery and neglect.
What I mean is, I may not be back here for a while,
But I'm glad I came. Dusk comes like a wolf
Through underbrush, sniffing the air for a kill.
I know this vibe, same in every city, so I gun
My rental hard. Near the onramp toward Chicago,
Stopped at a signal, a streetwalking woman
Starts to approach, then decides against it. Maybe
Something in my eyes turns her back. Maybe
My stare is approaching the thousandth yard.
She's out early, I think, the sky still pink
In some places, the whole boulevard a shade short
Of blood. *Streetwalking woman, sister of my soul.*
In the day's last light, she is almost beautiful.

MÍRALO

This poem
is a finger
pointing at
the moon.
Nevermind
the knuckles'
hundred nicks,
this chiseled history
of wrongheaded
scraps.
Ignore the stink
of bloodmusk,
every woman
touched, loved
or not, habits
held long or
let go. Míralo—
this poem is
a finger pointing
out, gnarled, up
at a blue
quarter moon,

a crater for each
earned misery,
the borrowed light
we live by.
This finger
is a poem,
wrinkled, scarred,
and dirty under
the nail, but
nevermind the grime,
mothafuck
my cuticles—
You big dummy,
don't look
at my finger—
I'm trying to
show you
the moon.

THE PRISONER'S WIFE

To touch him—where? Scapula? Vertebrae?—
I have to let him hear my voice first,
Hum something he knows. Make sure he's awake.
Been this way since he's back in the world.

I have to whisper soft as a child. First
Time I reached for him in the dark, I learned.
Like his first night home. In that world,
I imagine the shanks and showers, bigger men,

If they touched him. In the dark. I've learned
Not to ask. What fingers may have grazed his skin
Is not for me to know. Let me run this man a bath.
That he's even here is a miracle. Seven years

I've waited to glaze his fingers, his skin,
To sing his name until he learns it right. My risen,
Black Lazarus. Here. Seven summers, still intact.
Tonight, watch these nails cut wings into his back.

STOLEN STARLIGHT LOUNGE SUTRA

Yusef's Groove

Woman I got the blues
        xeroxed on brainmatter.
                Blues chanting hoodoo
Revival. Blasphemy for black hands
        men can't trust with wood.

Woman, we were almost
unreal. Uncertainty in blue. Twenty tunnels
between each bad step,
        unnatural death, and gypsy hangman,
Woman, we were almost unreal.

You try to beat loneliness,
        Blues chanting hoodoo revival

You try to beat loneliness,
        Uncertainty in blue

What counts up here, when moon cuts through,
        between each bad step, when the smoke house
        is a white horse casting shadows,

woman, what counts here is the cerulean ruckus,
  the nocturne tune in the background
of silence, the night muse
    of the little man

dancing naked in your memory cave,
    what counts here
is the little man dancing naked
    in your dream shredding machine.

This little man, looking
  a mad dog dead in the eyes,
    in the day's mirror,
      dances naked in insufficient

      blue light, not
      apologizing, not
      knowing better, not

turning from the hellhounds airbrushed
on horse-headed clouds, but facing the bounty
of black luster. Facing it. What counts,
        is you, woman. You
and the little man facing one another in the day's blue mirror,
        in uncertainty, through shredded dreams,

saying, "Here I am. (Here we are)
I can still sing. (We can still sing)"
What counts, woman,
        is you. You
and this little man
        facing one another.
                Singing. Still.

SOON I'LL BE LOVING YOU AGAIN

Picture the preacher's son   secular   sanctified
spotlight and nightsweat   bluesmoke and silkthroat
Eyes closed   head tossed   knees trembling
Trouble Man   moaning wholly   Holy
Love   Have mercy   Love have
mercy   holler   Marvin   holler

Dreamed of you this morning
then came the dawn and
I thought that you were here with me

Picture the poet   nightsweat and lamplight
fingers throbbing   threadbare tongue   ghost mounted
errant son   Picture the woman
known before   comes back   spoken for
See the poet's barren hands   blood before words
this bard without throat   a woman to bring back
and no song to sing   no song to sing
help me holler   Marvin   help me   help her   remember

Dreamed of you this morning
then came the dawn and
I thought that you were here with me

What is it   Marvin   makes a man
need so strong   what he ain't suppose to have
        want so bad   what he ain't suppose to want
what is it   Marvin   makes men like us   holler
        and moan   holler and moan   why a blues
so mean   she gotta come back twice

Dreamed of you this morning
        then came the dawn and
I thought that you were here with me

ROUND MIDNIGHT

Some nights I watch you
    sleep, the eyelids' jig

and beg, the blue rise
    of memory and moon.

When you drift, I snatch
    a machete from behind

a bedpost, stalk the night,
    plot the rise of infidels.

Before dawn, maybe you
    whisper the six histories

of river and rain, rise like
    steam from an open wound,

wrap yourself in ash,
    blood and honey.

Maybe you navigate
    stained glass streets,

havoc the avenues, ransack
 basilica in search of me.

Maybe you burn candles,
 moan canticles, conjure

lightning and thunderclap.
 Sweet river woman,

waist beaded and bangled,
 breathe moon and I will

dream too. Rise blue
 and I will find you.

FOR THE GOOD TIMES

A shadow splits the beam
under your door   clanks keys
you become wind
and waist beads
wrap a skirt
slide me out
to the fire escape

the ring on your finger
framed photo on the nightstand
say you his woman

your funk in my beard
the cold heft of a .38 in my palm
beg different

THE JUJU

Before we make love, you ask me again
To tell the story, something whispered
Years ago in another city, another woman's
Smoke in my ear. You want to hear
About Ghanaian sky, an open field,
A little girl humming lullabies at dusk.
How a hawk's wing brushed her shoulder,
Muscled a talon-snatched two year old
Into the dark. You like to hear about the juju,
Rumors of roots worked by a bad man's wife,
The savannah the mistress collapsed in,
Her baby's cries stretched like intestines
Across the sky. And when I tell you
What was told me, how after that day
Neither mistress nor child was ever seen,
How villagers say some nights
You can hear them rustling moonlight,
Your ring finger catches a shaft
Of curtain-cut neon, and I wonder
What juju will be told on us,
In which city, in whose dark.

SECOND LINE

At the corner of 149th Street and 3rd Ave., a young woman
Kisses tears from her baby's cheeks. Tears and rain.
Rain the weatherman missed catches a whole borough, and skin
Shimmers for blocks in each direction. The mother, on line
For the crosstown bus, shifts the child hip to hip, groans
Toward the sky. Curses the clouds, the wait, and every horn

Of every passing car this sunless afternoon—horns
Of gypsy cabs she can't afford, men who spot the woman
From behind and offer up vulgarities. Syncopated moans
Swell in the distance. And, she thinks, pots and pans—the rain
Playing tricks with the ear's tambourine—lines
Of cheap mascara scrambling down her own soft cheek.

And then she sees, hears them. Not pots and pans, but animal hides
Stretched taut and beat with sticks. And there are these . . . horns?
Yes, horns—tuba, trumpet, trombone—a crooked line
Of cornrows and Saints jerseys marching, women
Dancing beside them, up the block. A parade despite the rain.
To spite the rain. A wino rises to his feet, hums

Along, grinding his hips at a passing woman, moans
Again, but this time it's the music, not her rain-cool skin
That's got him singing, "Little Liza Jane," and rain
Puddles turn geyser under his shuffling feet. The horns
Wail and now the baby's smiling with both teeth. The mother
Smiles, too, mambos the baby on her hip. The drum line

Boogies past, vendors and passersby paused, or not, lined
Along both sides of the street, wondering what this means—
South Bronx Mardi Gras, sans beads and topless women,
Traffic stopped to let it through, a cart of skinned
Mangoes and oranges following close. A trucker leans into his horn
To keep time with the band, blowing through the rain.

"They're here from Katrina," the drunk calls out, as if the storm
Were a country unto itself, with its own government, borders,
And taxes. As if this would explain these ten young men, their brass
And bass kick rumbling toward the concourse. Not dirge,
But jubilee, and a hundred soaked shirts, bodies
Slick and writhing in rain—working men and women

Forgetting, for a spell, the work of being men and women, letting rain
And music wash over them, sinew and soul. The second line
Stretched, now, for blocks, and the Bronx all trumpet and moan.

SONG

after Adrian Matejka, Ernesto Mercer

I know it's wrong to stare, but it's Tuesday,
The express is going local, and this woman's

Thighs—cocoa-buttered, crossed, and stacked
To her chin—are the only beauty I think I'll see

For the next forty minutes. Not the train's
Muttering junkie, who pauses a little too long

In front of me, dozing, but never losing balance.
Not the rat we notice scurry past the closing doors,

Terrorizing the rush hour platform. Not
Even these five old Black men, harmonizing

About begging and pride, about a woman
Who won't come home. But skin, refracted

Light, and the hem's hard mysteries. I imagine
There's a man somewhere in this city, working

Up the nerve to beg this woman home, the sweet
Reconciliation of sweat on sweat, and pride

Not even afterthought. My own woman, who
I've begged sometimes not to leave, and begged

Sometimes please to leave, never has, also waits,
Uptown, in a fourth floor walk-up, in an old t-shirt

For me to make it back. She waits for me to come
Through jungles, over rivers, out from underground.

She waits, without fear, knowing no matter what,
I will make it home. And, God, there were times

I probably shouldn't have, but did, and lived
To see this day, the junkies, rats, and thighs,

And I say, praise it all. Even this ride, its every
Bump and stall, and each funky body pressed

To another, sweat earned over hours, bent over moats,
Caged in cubicles, and after it all, the pouring

Of us, like scotch, into daylight. Dusk.
Rush hour. This long trip home. Praise it all.

The dead miss out on summer. The sun
Bouncing off moving trains and a woman

To love you when you get inside. Somewhere
In this city, a man will plead for love gone,

Another chance, and think himself miserable.
He'll know, somewhere deep, he may never

Win her back. But he'll know, even deeper,
That there is a kind of joy in the begging

Itself, that all songs are love songs. Blues,
Especially. Praise the knowledge. Praise

The opening and closing doors, the ascent
Into light, heat, each sidewalk square, cracks

And all, the hundred and twelve stairs between
Lobby and my woman's front door, the exact

Moment, I let in this city, let out this sweat,
And come to own this mighty, mighty joy.

NOTES

"THE CORNER": "'Legba," or "Elegba," is the Yoruba Orisha often associated with crossroads, intersections, and destiny. Also known as Eshu, widely considered a trickster god.

"Hustle": "Soledad" refers to Soledad Correctional Training Facility (State prison), Salinas, CA.

"Variation on a Theme by Eazy E": Chuck Taylor Converse are inexpensive canvas sneakers popular among certain L.A. gang members and thug life aspirants in the 1980's.

"November 26, 1980": One of the greatest boxers of all time, Roberto Durán is famous for quitting the eighth round in his 1980 rematch with Sugar Ray Leonard. The imfamous phrase, "No mas, no mas," commonly attributed to Duran was actually spoken by ABC sports commentator, Howard Cosell.

"Dream Fragment with a Shot Clock and Whistles In It": In the summer of 1996, the Los Angeles Lakers acquired center, Shaquille O'Neal, then a free agent. The title borrows from a poem by Tony Trigilio.

"How to Split a Cold One": Olvera Street is an historic section of downtown Los Angeles, known for its festive Mexican marketplace, music and dance.

"Trouble Man": Title song of a soundtrack album of the same name, "Trouble Man," was written and recorded by Marvin Gaye, released in 1972.

"Flowers for Etheridge": Etheridge Knight (1931-1991) was an award winning African-American poet. Born in Corinth, Mississippi, he served in the Korean War, where a shrapnel wound led to an addiction to pain killing drugs, later heroin. Soon after his discharge from the army, Knight was sentenced to Indiana state prison for armed robbery. In prison, he began writing poetry. Among his most well-known books are *Poems from Prison, Belly Song,* and the American Book Award winning collection, *The Essential Etheridge Knight.* In March 1991, he died of lung cancer. Some of the lines in this poem allude to, converse with, or quote from, certain of Knight's better known poems. The poem, in general, is inspired by and in conversation with Larry Levis' poem, "Those Graves in Rome," which chronicles his trip to visit the grave of the English poet, John Keats. Section IV. of the poem mentions Mbembe Milton Smith, an African-American poet who died of an apparent suicide in 1982. Knight eulogized him in the poem, "A Black Poet Leaps to His Death."

"Stolen Starlight Lounge Sutra": This poem is a cento, comprised almost entirely of lines and titles from the index of *Pleasure Dome: New and Collected Poems of Yusef Komunyakaa*, Wesleyan Press, 2004.

"Soon I'll Be Loving You Again": Following the formal requirements of the "Bop" form, created by Afaa Michael Weaver at the Cave Canem Workshop, this poem includes song lyrics from "Soon I'll Be Loving You Again," written and performed by Marvin Gaye for his album, *I Want You*, released in 1976.

"Second Line": In traditional New Orleans parades, there is a "main line," consisting of the musicians and licensed marchers. The "Second Line" is composed of parade followers, dancers and other celebrants. It is tradition at some funerals in New Orleans for a band to play in subdued, mournful tones on the way to the funeral, and on the way from the burial, to play upbeat and jubilant music, while people dance hard to celebrate the life of the deceased. In 2007, a band of young New Orleans musicians, on tour to raise funds for victims of Hurricane Katrina, visited the South Bronx.

"Song": Was inspired by an unpublished poem by D.C. poet, Ernesto Mercer, and borrows from a line in Adrian Matejka's collection, *Mixology*, Penguin Books, 2009.

ACKNOWLEDGMENTS

MANY THANKS TO the following institutions for providing time, space, and other valuable resources, without which the completion of this project would have been impossible: Atlantic Center for the Arts, Cave Canem Foundation, Columbia College Chicago and the Elma P. Stuckey Visiting Emerging Poet-in-Residency (shout out to my Duende Crew), Fine Arts Work Center in Provincetown, Massachusetts, New York Times, New York University's Graduate Program in Creative Writing, Poets House NYC, Soul Mountain Retreat, Teachers and Writers Collaborative, VONA, and the Wisconsin Institute for Creative Writing, for the Jay C. and Ruth Halls Poetry Fellowship.

Thank you to my most generous mentors and teachers: Breyten Breytenbach, Toi Derricotte, Joel Dias-Porter, Cornelius Eady, Martín Espada, Kimiko Hahn, Brandon D. Johnson, Yusef Komunyakaa, Philip Levine, Sonia Sanchez, Susan Wheeler, and, of course, the outstanding faculty at Cave Canem.

Gargantuan thanks to the following individuals, who've read poems, lent money, shared smoke, given food or shelter, or otherwise held a brother down: Moms, first and foremost. Reginald Dwayne Betts, Tara Betts, Remica Bingham, Roger Bonair-Agard, Mahogany Brown, Jericho Brown, Sarah Browning, Christian Campbell, Russell Carmony, DeLána Dameron, Latasha Diggs, Baba Malik Duncan (and Ilé Ashé, Brooklyn), Quincy Flowers, Krista Franklin, Yolanda Franklin, Ross Gay, Regie Gibson, Aracelis Girmay, Yanira González, Jose Gouveia, Jonathan Gray, Rachel Eliza Griffiths, Julie Grigsby, Kelle Groom, Melissa Hammerle, Joseph Hayes, Donna Hernández, Michael Hinken, Lita Hooper, Randall Horton, Anoa Hunter, Marcus Jackson, Tyehimba Jess, Amaud Jamaul and Cherene Sherrard Johnson, Brian Jones, Janine Joseph, Michon Lartigue, Raina J. León, Marie-Elizabeth Mali, Allison Meyers, Ernesto Mercer, Nina Mercer, Dante Micheaux, Carolyn Micklem, Sarah Micklem, E. Ethelbert Miller, Sami Miranda, Coco Mitchell, Maurice Mitchell, Kamilah Aisha Moon, Sage Morgan-Hubbard, Marilyn Nelson, Lisa Pegram, Melissa Range, Patrick

Rosal, Salvatore Scibona, Patricia Smith, Sue Song, Samantha Thornhill, Plinio Trujillo, Yosara Trujillo, Ron Villanueva, Rich Villar, LouderArts/Acentos Familia, and the whole Cave Canem massive. ¡Estamos aquí!

Deep gratitude to Willie Perdomo and Lisa Simmons at Cypher Books for putting me on—and for putting up with my crazy ass. (Willie, yours was the voice that brought me to poetry in the first place. So I'm honored to be riding with you. For real.)

Another shout to Martín Espada for always being there, even when life happens.

Lastly, I have to thank the most loving, most patient, the ultimate ride-or-die—Donitra Clemons. Nothing I say here could do you justice. Your love is gangsta.

ABOUT THE AUTHOR

JOHN MURILLO is the current Jay C. and Ruth Halls Poetry Fellow at the Wisconsin Institute for Creative Writing. A graduate of New York University's MFA program in creative writing, he has also received fellowships from the Fine Arts Work Center in Provincetown, Massachusetts, Cave Canem, and the New York Times. He is a two-time Larry Neal Writers' Award winner and the inaugural Elma P. Stuckey Visiting Emerging Poet-in-Residence at Columbia College Chicago. His poetry has appeared in such publications as Callaloo, Court Green, Ploughshares, Ninth Letter, and the anthology, *Writing Self and Community: African-American Poetry After the Civil Rights Movement*. *Up Jump the Boogie* is his first collection.